{ CITIESCAPE }

SYDNEY*

{ CITIESCAPE }

MIRIAM RAPHAEL

CONTENTS*

VITAL STATS*

NAME Sydney **AKA** The Emerald City, Sin City
DATE OF BIRTH 26 January 1788, when Captain
Arthur Phillip landed the First Fleet at Sydney Cove
HEIGHT 42m **SIZE** 1800 sq km
HOME Australia
POPULATION 4 million

7.

PEOPLE*

{ }

* THE QUESTION 'WHERE ARE YOU FROM?' IS A STANDARD OPENING IN SYDNEY CONVERSATION. Ever since New South Wales (NSW) became self-governing in 1855, people have been lured to the city from more than 280 nations. Nearly a quarter of all Sydney residents speak a language other than English – 140 languages in total. Sydney also has the largest indigenous population of all Australian cities and the country's most vibrant gay and lesbian community.

SYDNEYSIDERS HAVE a strong work-hard/play-hard mentality, taking their jobs seriously but also making the most of the city's 300 sunny days a year with early morning surfs, mid-week barbecues and long sporting sessions on the weekends. Sydney's brand of hedonism entails open-air festivals, drinking in cocktails and views at the newest bar and spending the weekends soaking up the sun.

ANATOMY*

{ *THE HARBOUR DIVIDES SYDNEY INTO NORTHERN AND SOUTHERN HALVES, WITH THE SYDNEY HARBOUR BRIDGE AND THE HARBOUR TUNNEL JOINING THE two shores. Ferries service the waterside suburbs, arriving at Circular Quay to connect with the buses which plough through the long and narrow city centre from The Rocks in the north to Central Station in the south. }

THE CITY IS bounded by Hyde Park to the east and Darling Harbour to the west. East of the city centre are the inner-city suburbs Darlinghurst, Kings Cross and Paddington, which give way to the exclusive neighbourhoods of Double Bay and Vaucluse. The ocean beach suburbs start at Bondi and continue down south to Cronulla. West of the bridge are previously working-class but now gentrified suburbs like Pyrmont and Balmain. The inner west includes Newtown, with its large student population, and the Italian suburb Leichhardt. To the north and south the suburbs stretch 20 kilometres, their limits defined by national parks. The western suburbs sprawl to the Nepean River at the foothills of the Blue Mountains.

11.

PERSON ALITY*

{ *SYDNEY TODAY IS A BOLD, COLOURFUL, BRASSY, HEDONISTIC, SWAGGERINGLY BEAUTIFUL AND INTENSELY IDIOSYNCRATIC** destination. But two centuries ago the 11 ships and 1400 crew and convicts of the First Fleet, assembled by Arthur Phillip, only stayed a week in Botany Bay before deciding that it was a real-estate disaster. }

PHILLIP SAILED INTO Port Jackson (aka Sydney Harbour) on 26 January 1788, and erected tents at Circular Quay and the Rocks, under the cynical eye of passing French explorer La Pérouse. By the time La Pérouse had packed his baguettes and sailed away, the British were giving serious thought to abandoning the settlement and making for Norfolk Island. Obviously, they chose to persevere. Phillip established reasonable relations with the Eora tribe who occupied the area, and settlers concentrated on producing the wool which was to become an export staple. With the discovery of gold in the 1850s, immigration boomed and the city began to take shape.

13.

SYDNEY IS MOULDED by two things – its geography and its people. The deep-water harbour is surrounded by low tree-covered ridges, the ocean beaches are backed by craggy cliffs. The harbour gave Sydney wealth as a port, and still offers recreation and cooling breezes. Its twin icons, the Harbour Bridge and the Opera House, host or act as a backdrop for major community activities.

AT THE SAME TIME, every resident has their own Sydney, an area where they grew up and to which they feel they belong. It's a city of immigrants. The first, tentative waves of immigration following the First Fleet began to grow larger as disasters in Europe and increasing wealth and independence in the antipodes made relocation more appealing. But it was the immigration boom that began post-war – and continues today – that gives Sydney its cultural diversity. The first wave of immigrants was made up of people from 'old Europe' seeking refuge from the scars of conflict; the next wave was from the Middle East; the most recent arrivals are from Southeast Asia.

THEY'VE ALL made their cultures visible in the cityscape. There's the golden tree in Chinatown, the mosque at Lakemba, the pastiche of Sienna in Leichhardt and the little Dizengov that is Hall Street Bondi. A walk down Cleveland Street in Surry Hills will take you to India, chasing at the heels of Turkey to Lebanon, by way of Japan. Twenty years ago you'd have found 40 styles of food in Sydney – today there are over 100.

THE CHAPTERS THAT follow offer a slice of Sydney's rich cream-cake persona – swinging, succulent, kooky, escapist, and daring you to indulge in a large helping!

SWINGING*

{ }

*SYDNEY IS A TOWN THAT LIVES EQUALLY FOR WORK AND FOR PLEASURE.** After the long hours in the offices, shops, bars and cafés are done, Sydney is a party town – especially when the nights are balmy (which is at least half the year).

YOU CAN FIND Sydneysiders dotting the cafés around town – this is a city that runs on excellent Italian coffee. Filling out the days might involve hitting the markets of Surry Hills, Paddington or Bondi or dipping in and out of the strips of boutiques that run through the inner suburbs, and stopping to refuel at any number of tasty food and drink stops. Cooking up a feast for friends is a favourite weekend pastime, often after a trip to the fish markets or to Paddy's for fresh produce, or maybe using new and exotic ingredients picked up at a farmers' market or chaotic Asian supermarket.

HARDLY A WEEK goes by without a celebration of some kind. Whether it's massive rock festivals held at the Olympic complex or outdoor dance parties at some of the

17.

city's naturally beautiful locales – the Domain, Centennial Park or Bondi Beach – the people of Sydney love to come together en masse for music, art, food and movies.

AT NIGHT the streets of the inner suburbs fill with revellers; drinkers and club-goers wander up and down Oxford Street or into Kings Cross to wait in line in front of their favourite nightspot until they're deemed cool enough to enter. At the end of the night (or morning) they stumble out past dodgy kebab stands and groups of bikers on their way home.

IN THE CITY PROPER, groups of young people wander around from bar to bar among the empty skyscrapers, and finish the night chowing down at fast-food outlets before catching the last train back to the suburbs. The bars at King Street Wharf and Cockle Bay attract the suits; travellers prefer the circuit of international bars and Irish pubs, with their 24-hour liquor licences, Miss Backpacker contests and satellite sports broadcasts. Come St Patrick's Day, of course, they all add an 'O' to their surname and head to The Rocks to get blotto on Guinness.

LOCAL HIPSTERS and music lovers gather in the pubs around Central and in Surry Hills – it's not uncommon to see a gaggle of Goths wandering past a bemused group of Asian tourists. These inner-city venues heave with crowds eager to hear the latest live talent and the sounds of homespun rock and roll. When late-night hunger hits it's time for a $5 steak at a pub bistro or salt-and-pepper squid in Chinatown, followed maybe by a wander past the brothels and swingers' venues in Surry Hills to a packed karaoke joint in the Cross – which, like the rest of the city, is open all night.

SHIMMY FOR YOUR RIGHTS*

{ *SYDNEY LOVES A PARTY AND THEY DON'T COME ANY BIGGER THAN THE ANNUAL JOYFUL HEDONISM-MEETS-POLITICAL-PROTEST** Gay and Lesbian Mardi Gras parade along Oxford Street. The culmination of a month of colourful, sequined festival madness – including a sports carnival, a film festival, theatre performances and lots of parties – the parade kicks off with the roar of Dykes on Bikes, the famed lesbian motorcycle club. Their Harleys and Hondas are followed by more than 6000 people strutting, dancing, skipping, riding and shimmying their way down the Great White Way (Oxford Street) in the name of tradition, celebration and protest. }

THE PARADE BEGAN as a civil rights demonstration in 1978 (when dozens of marchers were arrested), and has become renowned for its hundreds of spectacular floats, which often make witty comment on the political climate of the time. It's the world's largest night-time costume parade and attracts thousands of international visitors, not to mention over half a million Sydneysiders jostling for prime positions atop milk crates along Oxford Street.

21.

GIVEN THE CITY'S ADORATION
of the body beautiful, it's only
natural that Sydney has a vital
dance culture. Taylor Square on
Oxford Street – the original gay
ghetto of the 1980s – reverberates
to the mundane sounds of heavy
traffic and roadworks by day, but it's
thriving by night when the city's
queers come out to play. Sculpted
torsos bump and grind their way
from the bar to the dance floor and
back, while podium dancers go-go
with zeal – unlike the punters, their
shirts stay on.

DIRTY DANCING*

*IT'S DIRTY, IT'S FUN AND IT'S FRIVOLOUS. SYDNEY GOES WILD FOR A BIT OF BURLESQUE.** Salubrious old-world cabaret meets sophisticated salon as artists deliver an explosive mix of circus, vaudeville, striptease and performance art.

THE MONTHLY SELL-OUT event Gurlesque, for example, is a glorious in-your-face romp with raunchy routines and lavish costumes: what else would you expect from two performers named Sex Intents and Glita Supernova? It's Sydney's only lesbian strip-show.

FOR THOSE WANTING their own solo, Lola the Vamp runs Friday-night classes on how to bump and grind for performance or pleasure. Work on your feline strut, shimmy, shake and twitter the ostrich-feather fans. But it's not all about tassle-twirling. At its heart, burlesque is about the tension between the hidden and the revealed, and the interaction between dancer and audience.

SYDNEY FESTIVAL*

{ *** COMPARED WITH THE LONG-ESTABLISHED PERTH AND ADELAIDE FESTIVALS, THE SYDNEY CELEBRATION –** which didn't get started until 1977 – was always going to be criticised as brash and lightweight. Its reputation wasn't helped in the early years by a programme that offered anything and everything – vintage car rallies, face-painting, kite-flying, bocce, dog obedience trials and Chinese scarf dancing. }

THESE DAYS, the Sydney Festival's three-week cultural extravaganza, held during hot and balmy January, is one of the highlights of summer. Packed programmes of local and international theatre, music, dance, multidisciplinary and visual arts might feature the Guangdong Acrobats of China, perhaps, followed by Elvis Costello playing with the Sydney Symphony Orchestra. It's probably Australia's largest cultural happening and has been acclaimed as the city's favourite annual event. The free outdoor concerts like Jazz in the Domain attract enormous crowds (up to 85,000 people), while others at Darling Harbour and on the forecourt of the Opera House create a fabulous buzz.

27.

FOR OVER 40,000 YEARS,
Indigenous Australians have
used dance and song to celebrate,
mourn and tell stories about the
land, their communities and their
ways of life. Some dances and
songs are sacred or secret, and
many tell the stories of Ancestral
Beings and the Dreamtime (a key
concept in the spirituality of
mainland Aboriginal cultures).

THE FAKE AND THE FABULOUS*

{ *IT MAY BE THE WEATHER OR A REACTION TO THE SURPLUS OF MALLS AND GLITZY BOUTIQUES,** but visiting the weekend markets is a must for many Sydney-siders. At Paddy's Markets, in the heart of Chinatown, locals push their way through the hordes for the cheapest deals on everything from live budgies (birds) to board games and mobile phones. Three pairs of fake Gucci sunglasses later, you'll still have enough cash for a week's worth of fresh veggies and a bag of prawns. }

THERE'S NOTHING FAKE about the merchandise at Kirribilli Market, a popular haunt with the fashion set, who loudly assess its vintage wares. The competition is keen – cast a glance at the stunning harbour views and someone may snap up the pair of second-hand boots you've been admiring.

ACROSS TOWN in the Bondi Markets on a Sunday, beautiful girls wearing little more than sunglasses and a postage-stamp-size bikini queue for the sausage sizzle, while young surfers circle the market stalls on a quest for the perfect piece of retro furniture.

31.

SYDNEY SWANS *

{ *GRAB THAT SCARF AND FOLLOW THE SWARM OF AUSSIE RULES FOOTBALL
LOVERS AS THEY START THEIR MARCH THROUGH PADDINGTON to the home of
the Swans, the Sydney Cricket Ground. And as the players storm the 3.5-metre-high
banner, 'Cheer, Cheer the Red and the White'! }

AUSTRALIAN RULES Football (aka AFL) is the most-watched sport in the country. It's
fast, it's aggressive, and though Sydney is traditionally a rugby town, every year the 10
home games of its beloved high-flying Swans attract a crowd of 40,000 each. In 2005,
the South Melbourne-turned-Sydney club won its first premiership flag in 72 years – in
spite of history, logic, a better credentialled opposition and the critics. From 10 points
down in the game's last quarter, the Swans fought back to win by four points, in front
of 91,898 fans at the Melbourne Cricket Ground (better known as the MCG). It will go
down as a great AFL grand final.

THE DOMAIN *

{ *IT'S 3PM AND YOU'RE STANDING IN THE MIDDLE OF THE DOMAIN WITH A SIX-PACK UNDER ONE ARM AND A BAGUETTE UNDER THE OTHER,** lost in a sea of slightly sozzled Sydneysiders, who've been feasting on Camembert and Chardonnay since dawn. It's at this point you realise that no matter how early you get to a free event in Sydney – be it Jazz in the Domain, Tropfest or Symphony under the Stars – there will always be many who got there earlier. }

THE DOMAIN was set aside in 1788 by Governor Phillip as his private reserve and over the years became a popular site for political protests. These days, the crowds are mostly on less demanding missions. Jazz in the Domain and Symphony under the Stars are both part of the January Sydney Festival and attract crowds of thousands keen to hear top local and international musicians. Tropfest, the world's largest short-film festival, is also held here each February.

SUCCU LENT *

{ * **AUSTRALIAN CUISINE HAS COME A LONG WAY FROM THE MEAT-AND-THREE-VEG OF ITS BRITISH ROOTS.** Multicultural inspirations, stellar produce and bold flavours are the cornerstones of Mod Oz (Modern Australian) cooking, helped along by a dining public prepared to experiment. }

SYDNEY IS a dining destination worth the flight. The iconic meal is (arguably) a plate of sweet, plump rock oysters or prawns in a seat looking out over the harbour, with the sun behind you and a bottle of chilled white wine at your side. And if you're feeling a little jaded about life in the Emerald City, a killer martini tastes even better with an eye-ful of the Opera House; in the Bondi breeze, a caipiroska is perfect. A perfect Sunday is watching the sun sink over the harbour with good friends and some cold beers.

OF COURSE, such great views usually come with a price – unless you pack a hamper and a cold bottle from home. Sydneysiders like nothing more than taking advantage of their glorious weather for a weekend picnic with friends. They'll find a spot in one of the many parks on the water (think McKell or Long Nose Point) and settle in for a long afternoon with spread blankets for the babies and a football for the kids. Evening brings wisps of smoke and the whiff of onions rising from the many beach-side barbecues, as snags (sausages), T-bone steaks and kebabs are char-grilled to taste.

FEW PLACES in the world can match Australian seafood. The prawns are succulent, the crayfish and Balmain bugs sweet, the mussels are fit for any mariner and the fish gleam with freshness: so many varieties and so many names!

FARMERS, PRODUCERS AND CHEFS are passionate about making the city a great place for food. There are regular produce markets all around the city, from Chinatown to Fox Studios, from Pyrmont to Cabramatta, and in restaurant kitchens a new delicacy is invented – or reinvented – almost every week. And as in all major cities, architects fall over themselves to come up with the most novel ideas in restaurant design. Taking inspiration from the water, using old timbers and new metals, incorporating open preparation and cooking areas, going intimate or communal, setting up for fine dining or alfresco – nothing is off limits.

COFFEE CULTURE*

{ *IN A TOWN WHERE STATUS IS KING, NOBODY WIELDS MORE POWER THAN THE }
BARISTAS WHO WORK THE ESPRESSO MACHINES at Sydney's top coffee haunts. From the established caffeine strips of Darlinghurst in the east to Little Italy (Leichhardt) in the inner west, they preside over the hissing machines and rumbling grinders. A wait for an early-morning caffe latte can turn into a lesson in coffee culture from an enthusiastic barista.

FORGET THE STANDARD Sydney topics of real estate, the traffic and real estate – café conversation focuses on the perfect grind and why espresso should pour in a thin 30-second stream, or on the merits of Fair Trade versus coffee without a conscience. Though most coffee is still imported, Australian plantations (particularly those in northern New South Wales) are now starting to grow coffee that is competing well against overseas blends. Local coffee is all Arabica, a species that grows on the high plains and develops to a better quality. Australian coffee is known for its full body and sweet chocolate-caramel character.

PULL UP TO HARRY'S CAFE DE WHEELS AT WOOLLOOMOOLOO at 3am and it seems the whole street is hunched over their car bonnets scoffing Harry's famous chunky meat pies and mushy peas with a dollop of mash and a squirt of tomato sauce. This 24-hour pie cart has been an institution for sailors, politicians, cabbies and late-night revellers since 1945. It's one of the few pie carts in the world to be a tourist attraction, and the photos prove that anyone and everyone comes to Harry's – even Pamela Anderson. Of course, it may not be the food that's the attraction. After all, pies and mushy peas? You're not talking gourmet here… although the food does happen to come with million-dollar water views.

FISHY BUSINESS*

{ *FOLLOW YOUR NOSE TO THE SYDNEY FISH MARKET IN BLACKWATTLE BAY: IT'S THE BIGGEST IN THE SOUTHERN HEMISPHERE, selling 15 million kilograms of seafood each year and offering over 100 different species each day. Stroll and slip your way around the wet fish counters to pick up the day's meal, then queue at a hot grill for a seafood platter of squid, fish, mussels and chips – you'll have to fight other diners and the seagulls for a table outside. }

ALTERNATIVELY, TAKE a guided tour, visit the crab cages, learn how to make a Thai kingfish curry, or take a class on the best way to throw another shrimp on the barbie. Behind the scenes, the early-morning fish auctions are blindingly fast-paced as wholesalers take their pick of all that glorious seafood using a computerised auction system.

WHETHER YOU'RE AFTER live sea urchin for home-made sushi, a still-thrashing Balmain bug or a dozen freshly shucked Sydney rock oysters, this is one piscatorial paradise.

BANKSTOWN*

{ *ONE OF THE BEST PLACES IN SYDNEY TO GET THE TASTE BUDS DANCING IS }
BANKSTOWN, approximately 20 kilometres to the southwest of the central business district, out with the velodrome for the Olympic cycling events. It's the city's least recognised but fastest-growing food areas.

TRAWL THE PLAZAS for a freshly squeezed sugar-cane drink, pho and bun (noodle) soups from the south and north of Vietnam and food from street stalls. Buy live fish from tanks, Vietnamese pastries, pristine Asian greens and all manner of groceries. Ogle seasonal tropical fruit such as jackfruit, durian, and dragon fruit.

BANKSTOWN'S Lebanese pastry shops are presided over by master confectioners who turn pistachios, diced walnuts and filo pastry into works of art. The rectangles of chewy Syrian nougat are too delicious not to eat on the spot! And it's difficult to choose between pork vela and orange sausages from the Greek island of Lesvos or Macedonian svarci (fresh pork crackling)… but who can go past a tin of Latvian sprats?

47.

CHINATOWN*

{ *IF YOU WEAVE IN AND OUT OF CHINATOWN'S LATE-NIGHT MARKETS, YOU CAN SAVOUR THE PUNGENT TASTES AND SMELLS: a jumbled aroma of dried salted plums, stinky durian and swinging slabs of roasted pork and duck. In Sydney, where neighbourhoods often melt into one another without warning, Chinatown, with its city-that-never-sleeps hours and frantic energy, stands out like a spiky rambutan in a display of Granny Smith apples. }

AS OFFICE BUILDINGS give way to narrow, crowded alleys lined with bakers, butcher shops and windows filled with Hello Kitty and Pochacco, Japanese hipsters slurp on bubble tea, grocers rearrange their lychees and mangoes, and extended families wait patiently for a yum cha table.

IT'S NOT SURPRISING that this favoured haunt pulls huge crowds, especially at Chinese New Year when it puts on the most spectacular Lunar celebrations outside Asia. It's hard to get a table for a bowl of congee around here even at two in the morning.

A TASTE OF
THE MIDDLE EAST*

{ *** IN SYDNEY, IT'S PERFECTLY POSSIBLE TO SUBMERGE YOURSELF IN THE MAGIC OF THE MIDDLE EAST.** In Auburn there are confectioners offering juicy, sugar-dusted morsels of Turkish delight, halal butchers and supermarkets bursting with the spices of Asia Minor. Look for 'Turkish Viagra', shelled walnuts strung together and dipped in grape paste. }

TINY HOLE-IN-THE-WALL bakeries turn out fluffy slabs of Afghani flatbread. If you can go past the fresh Turkish bread strewn with sesame seeds, there are ovens filled with cheese-and-spinach-stuffed parcels and rounds of pizza dough doused with olive oil and za'atar (a spice blend).

ACROSS TOWN in Bondi, locals sit in the sun outside the Israeli-run felafel outlets, gorging themselves on shwarma, hummus, baba ghanouj and salad, all wiped up with still-warm pitta bread. For the complete shoes-off, cushion room Arabian experience, head to Cleveland Street in central Surry Hills or out to Bankstown in the west, where groups of friends get together for a big night of belly dancing, shisha-pipe smoking and live music.

KOOKY*

SYDNEY IS NOT KNOWN FOR ITS SUBTLETY. UNLIKE MANY OTHER CITIES, where bars and galleries may be tucked away in side streets or alleyways, everything in Sydney is on the surface. If you have to look hard for a restaurant it means it had to settle for a bad position; if a bar has mood lighting and couches it's 'dingy'; and if a nightclub has been open for six months it's dead.

THE TOWN has had to put up with its fair share of dumb blonde jokes, but don't judge a city by its façade. It also has a weirder side: there's the feeding of the lettuce to the giant dragon on Chinese New Year and tours of colonial streams and haunted quarantine centres; or go down to North Bondi and take in the spectacle of enormous bodybuilders perched next to elderly central European couples with their own deckchairs and umbrellas.

YOU CAN SLEEP over at the city zoo or watch the bats flying from the North Shore to Centennial Park – clap your hands to (supposedly) trick them into changing direction.

There are Water Rats too: the little furry type scurry across waterside roads; the big kind, aka the Harbour Police, scurry after drunken hoons.

SYDNEY TENDS to be regarded as the show pony of Australian cities, and when she's good she's very, very good, but when she's bad she's horrid. Beneath the successful multicultural metropolis with its dazzling harbour and shiny surfaces is a darker heart, a fascinating but bloody history. Every town has a dark side, but Sydney is good at hiding it – even during 'the best Olympics ever', not many visitors saw the humps put in the bus shelters to prevent the homeless from bedding down.

IT CAN BE a place of polarities and divisions, helped along by the hilly, winding geography. You can maintain an entirely separate existence in Sydney, and never engage with the other half or even with your neighbour. Home to the very rich and very poor, the very straight and the very gay, and the very quiet and the very loud, Sydney is most certainly not forgettable.

SCULPTURE
BY THE SEA*

{ *ALREADY ONE OF THE MOST SPECTACULAR AREAS IN SYDNEY, THE BONDI-TO-COOGEE COASTAL WALK** also becomes the world's largest outdoor sculpture gallery each November, when Sculpture by the Sea brings contemporary art to the coastline. Hundreds of amazing works by artists from Australia and abroad dot the cliffs, parks and beaches; the exhibition is one of the most popular outdoor events in the country. }

THE WALK ITSELF is worth a trip on its own merits. Aboriginal rock engravings make a fascinating detour from the panoramic views and soft-sanded beaches, or you can stop to watch the odd musical performance or a spontaneous game of frisbee in the park. After the two-hour stroll past historic seaside swimming pools, ultra-charming rock pools, and the parklands and reserves spread between the beaches and bays, you'll have worked up enough of an appetite to fully appreciate one of the many cafés along the way.

KINGS CROSS *

* THE LASCIVIOUS PAINTER DONALD FRIEND WAS ATTRACTED TO KINGS CROSS IN THE 1940s for its 'genuine Berlin air… where everybody is wicked'. Comparable with Paris's Montmartre if only because it's at the city's highest point, the Cross was seen by suburban Australia as crowded, seedy and depraved from its earliest days. But with the bright lights and the never-ending party of its scruffy cafés, cavernous jazz clubs and live theatre, it was a natural home for the city's artists, actors and writers.

TODAY THE CROSS is a cocktail of strip joints, prostitution, crime and drugs, shaken and stirred, but is nevertheless regarded with genuine affection by Sydneysiders. Locals fought tooth and nail to save the wonderful American-style neon signs of the clubs and bars which sprang up along the main drag – Showgirls, Stripperama, Porkies, the Pleasure Chest and Love Machine, and crowning all, the Coca-Cola sign dominating William Street.

SYDNEY ROCKS*

{ *AUSTRALIA WAS BORN AT THE ROCKS, WHERE SEWERS WERE OPEN AND }
RESIDENTS, CONVICTS, OFFICERS, WHALERS, SAILORS and street gangs were
raucous. It was the colony's maritime and commercial area, with warehouses and bond
stores, brothels and inns. Today's restored buildings and lanes hold the last hints of the
old community. They were almost demolished in the 1960s and '70s, only saved by
green bans in 1971 and a residents' barricade in 1975.

SYDNEY WAS UNITED by the Sydney Harbour Bridge, nicknamed 'the Coat Hanger'.
The largest and heaviest steel arch in the world, it's dear to residents' hearts for its
sheer size, simplicity and symmetry.

ONE OF THE DEFINING architectural moments of the 20th century – the Sydney
Opera House – was bequeathed to Sydney by Danish architect Jørn Utzon. Many
consider it the most beautiful – and iconic – of all Australian buildings.

ETERNITY*

{ ***SYDNEY ENTERED THE NEW MILLENNIUM IN A SHOWER OF PYROTECHNICS THAT FORMED THE WORD 'ETERNITY' ACROSS THE HARBOUR BRIDGE.** Symbolising the city's capacity for reinvention and hope for the future, the display had a special significance for Sydneysiders. From the early 1930s the word 'eternity' would appear mysteriously in yellow chalk on pavements around the city, written in a languid copperplate script. For 30 years there were some 50 new eternities every day. }

AFTER YEARS of speculation, *The Sunday Telegraph* revealed in 1956 that they were the work of Arthur Stace, a reformed alcoholic who had turned his life around in 1930 after hearing English evangelist John Ridley say 'Eternity! Eternity! Oh, that this word could be emblazoned across the streets of Sydney!'

THE CHALKED WORD was a Sydney institution until Stace's death in 1967 at age 83; his work now lives on in a brass replica of the word in Town Hall Square. It still makes passers-by stop, think and feel.

65.

END OF THE LINE*

{ *** WITH ITS GOTHIC BELLCOTE (WHICH MYSTERIOUSLY HAS NO BELL) AND WHIS-
PERS OF PSYCHIC HAPPENINGS,** the Sydney Central Mortuary Station is a real
inner-city hair-raiser even in broad daylight. The sandstone 'Necropolis Receiving
House', designed by colonial architect James Barnett, served the funeral trains between
Sydney and Rookwood Cemetery from 1867 until 1948. }

THE STATION STOOD near the original Central Station, called Sydney Terminal, which
had been built in 1855 for the run between Parramatta and Sydney. The very ugly look
of the second Sydney Terminal was the result of several awful additions at different
times in various cheap materials. Today's Central Station, the third station, was built in
stages. Eleven stonemasons commenced work on it in August 1902 and work gangs
demolished the platforms of the old Sydney Station as the new ones were built. The
clock tower and top two floors were completed in 1921 and the electric platforms
(numbers 16 to 23) and electric suburban rail network opened in 1926.

HIDDEN TREASURES *

{ *** THERE ARE MANY WAYS TO SEE SYDNEY, BUT ONE OF THE MORE UNUSUAL IS FROM TEN STORIES BELOW GROUND IN A STORMWATER DRAIN.** Underground urban exploration is about the thrill of exploiting the labyrinth of waterways, abandoned power stations, secret doorways and train tunnels – built and all but forgotten. In underground Sydney you never know what's around the next bend. }

IT'S ABOUT GETTING into a manhole at Central Station, walking up a brick oviform tunnel built in 1855 to Crown Street, then going under a 3-metre-high convict-built sandstone arch and along the overflow drains with their waterspouts and side passages to emerge at the base of the Opera House.

DRAIN-WATER RAFTING can take you from Hyde Park to Darling Harbour in less time than it takes to climb the stairs to the monorail station; of course, rain and an inflatable rubber boat are must-haves.

ZOO
WITH A VIEW*

{ *A DEFINITE SYDNEY HIGHLIGHT, EXCEPTIONAL TARONGA PARK ZOO BOASTS A SPECTACULAR LOCATION ON A HILLSIDE WITH GRAND VIEWS.** The zoo is home to over 3000 furred, scaled and feathered critters, usually in natural open enclosures so spread out that visitors get a healthy work-out trekking up and down the hill looking for them. A favourite is the platypus habitat, in which day and night have been switched so that the nocturnal beasts are active during opening hours. Other special treats are the much-loved koala and giraffe displays, the seal and bird shows, and the new rain-forest home of the Asian elephant. }

THE ZOO OFFERS a 'Roar & Snore' package: be awakened by the roar of the lions at the wildest slumber party around! The package begins with a safari to get a nocturnal peek at the animals as they relax after their daytime duties. You then fall asleep in a dome tent pitched under the stars and rise to the warbles, rumbles, squeaks, growls and roars of the animals greeting the day.

ESCAPIST *

{ }

A UNIQUE QUALITY OF SYDNEY IS THAT IT ALLOWS THOSE WHO CALL IT HOME TO ESCAPE BOTH OUT OF AND INTO THE CITY. Townspeople who run on long days of work and nights of hectic play need to stop, refresh and escape regularly to keep up with the pace. Some escape geographically, some mentally, and some in physical pursuits. Sydney gives them scope for all these activities.

THE VICTORIAN ERA gave the city the gardens of Hyde Park, the Domain and, most ambitiously, Centennial Park – such was the disdain for the native flora at the former 'Sydney Common', comprising some hundreds of acres, that was deforested, levelled and replanted. In the gardens and parks you can join in a pick-up game of soccer or cricket, or bring down a net for volleyball.

LESS ENERGETIC residents make the water their playground and jump on a ferry, stopping off at breathtaking spots in Middle Harbour or for fish and chips at Balmoral Beach or Manly. Others take in outdoor cinema, the city's vibrant visual arts or the burgeoning live music scene, or settle into the city's drinking dens – one of the most appealing and comfortable is the Art Deco Hollywood Hotel, owned by real-life movie star Doris Goddard. With its lazily spinning mirror ball, faded opulence and eccentric performers banging it out on the front-bar stage, the Hollywood is one of Sydney's last bastions of shabby elegance.

LUNCHTIME ESCAPES? For those lucky enough to live in Sydney, it offers a multitude of options for slipping away. The Chinese and Botanic Gardens are oases in the central business district; the Domain is often filled with personal trainers shouting at their sweaty clients. More relaxing is a stroll from the State Library to the Art Gallery of New South Wales, or down to Circular Quay and around to the more cutting-edge Museum of Contemporary Art. Sun-lovers head to Tamarama beach to see and be seen, and share the sand with the beautiful people. The more daring go au naturel at Lady Jane beach.

SYDNEYSIDERS ALSO EMBRACE the mini-break with a vengeance. In Palm Beach, separated from the city by winding beaches, you can walk the dunes and swim with some of Sydney's wealthiest citizens. Southward down the Bulli Pass, the less luxurious Thirroul has equally wild beaches huddled beneath a dramatic bushland escarpment. Or follow the compass west up into the expansive Blue Mountains, where the temperatures drop just enough for you to enjoy your bottle of red wine in front of the perfect cottage's open fire. Afterwards, take a bushwalk to fill your lungs with eucalyptus-scented air and your eyes with sweeping views of ancient rock formations and trees without end.

AUSSIEWOOD*

* WHEN THE CITY'S LIVE MUSIC SCENE CAME UNDER THREAT FROM THE 'POKIE INVASION' (the spread of poker machines), Sydneysiders threw their hands up in the air and said in their wonderfully fickle way, 'Well, at least we still have Aussiewood.' Since Rupert Murdoch opened Fox Studios Australia in 1988, the city has produced a stream of international hit flicks. *The Matrix* trilogy was filmed in Sydney, along with *Mission Impossible II* and several *Star Wars* features. There's a lot of love for the movie business in this town, and a lot of local actors eager to score supporting roles alongside Hollywood A-listers.

SYDNEY'S PASSION for film means that as well as the usual megaplexes there are several excellent art-house venues where locals can check out the newest foreign offerings. Movie buffs eagerly await the annual Sydney Film Festival, which was started in 1950 and is now a high-profile event featuring up to 250 films in two weeks. The city's diverse ethnic mix means that the Jewish, French and Greek film festivals are also incredibly popular.

77.

BEACH BUFFS*

{ ***THERE ARE FEW PLACES IN THE WORLD WHERE YOU CAN CATCH A BUS IN THE CENTRAL BUSINESS DISTRICT TO A WORLD-FAMOUS BEACH,** or where you can catch a wave first thing in the morning, at lunch and after work (depending on the surf). With about 50 beaches, Sydney has a new strip of sand for almost every week of the year. }

WHETHER THEY'RE SPREADING out a picnic at Neilsen Park, fossicking in the rock pools at Cronulla or diving under the crashing breakers at Manly, for Sydneysiders there's nothing more refreshing or relaxing than escaping to the beach.

LOCALS KNOW THAT floating off Camp Cove is the best way to experience the city skyline, and that it's worth the trek to Maroubra for the early morning waves. They see Bondi as the grande dame of beaches, with a majesty all its own and a healthy amount of decrepit charm, and reckon that snorkelling in the sun at beautiful Gordon's Bay is as good as a tropical island holiday any day.

IT'S THE FIRST SUNDAY IN MAY and the members of the Bondi Icebergs winter swim club are lined up at the edge of the ocean pool for the season's opening ceremony. It's raining and waves are crashing across the rocks but the swimmers, all wearing a polar bear logo, throw blocks of ice into the water and observe a minute's silence for deceased members. This strange ritual has been performed since 1929, and will continue as long as hundreds of locals are willing to brave the freezing water every week from May until the end of September.

LIFE-SAVERS*

{ ***ONE MINUTE YOU'RE SPLASHING IN THE SURF, THE NEXT YOU'RE KNOCKED FLAT BY A DUMPER.** You try to surface and take a breath, only to have another wave crash on top of you. Fortunately, Sydney's famed surf life-savers are there to drag you out of danger, wearing their red and yellow caps and one-size-too-small budgie smugglers (swimming briefs) or swimsuits. It's not all about bronzed bravado: more than 500,000 lives have been saved since the original surf life-saving association was formed in 1907; 8290 swimmers were rescued in 2005. }

AUSTRALIA WAS ONE of the first places in the world to have surf life-saving clubs, and the surf life-saver is respected throughout the country. In New South Wales alone, volunteers spend more than 270,000 hours patrolling 129 beaches along the mid-east coast each year – and despite life-saving's macho image, many life-savers are female. As well as saving people, the clubs organise championships, premierships, endurance races, surf lessons, festivals, lifeguard and life-saving training, first-aid classes and surf carnivals.

BACK IN SEPTEMBER 1902,
Mr William Gocher defied the law of the time and went bathing during prohibited hours (ie in daylight) at Manly Beach. His action, and similar acts by others that year, forced the legalisation of daylight bathing – allowing the pastime of surfing to become part of the national culture. Surf gurus name Manly, Dee Why and Cronulla as some of the top spots for waves in Sydney. Whichever beach you choose, you can always depend on getting sand dumped in your every crevice.

WATER VIEWS*

* IN A CITY THAT IS GETTING MORE EXPENSIVE BY THE DAY, ONE OF SYDNEY'S MOST PLEASURABLE EXPERIENCES COSTS A MERE FIVE DOLLARS. Jump aboard a yellow harbour ferry: the water churns, the spray wets your face and there's a nervous excitement about weaving around the sleek yachts, bobbing dinghies and Onassis-size cruisers. Head up the river or out towards Sydney Heads: from one end of the ferry the city skyline rises behind the Cahill Expressway, from the other the grey iron curve of the Coat Hanger soars in its full glory.

THE FERRIES have a pretty good reputation for reliability, cleanliness and flotation, (flotation is something of a priority). Many Sydneysiders use ferries to commute, so there are frequent services between early morning and midnight stopping at great locations like Darling Harbour, Balmain and Parramatta to the west, Kirribilli, Neutral Bay, Taronga Park Zoo and Manly on the North Shore and Double Bay in the east.

BENEATH THE SWEEP of the Anzac Bridge, 20 determined paddlers row to the steady beat of a drum. It's the Tsunami Dragon Boat Club, which trains in Blackwattle Bay three times a week in their long, flat-bottomed fibreglass boat with its ferocious-looking dragon's head and tail. The crew of accountants, academics and IT boffins will tell you that 'serious fun' is their motto.

90.

GOLD STAR

A STAR GOES TO SYDNEY FOR
HAVING FOOD FROM ALL AROUND
THE WORLD TOGETHER IN ONE
SUBURB OR ON ONE STREET.
THE CITY'S INFLUX OF IMMIGRANTS
MEAN YOU CAN GET EVERYTHING
FROM LAKSA TO INJERA.
SURE THERE'S ITALIAN AND
FRENCH, THAI AND MODERN ASIAN,
BUT THERE'S ALSO AFRICAN –
NORTH, SOUTH, EAST AND WEST.

MY PERFECT DAY

MIRIAM RAPHAEL

{ * Start the day with an early morning surf or swim down at Bronte, followed by a stroll along the cliffs of the famous coastal walk. Take in the Bondi scene over a fresh juice and an egg-white omelette (this is Sydney!) before heading to Paddington for some boutique browsing. From there, wander down Oxford Street into town and check out the free exhibitions at the Museum of Contemporary Art, along with its jaw-dropping harbour views. Lunch is up to you – yum cha in Chinatown or rock oysters at the Sydney Fish Market? Beer o'clock and it's time to find a pub with a garden or a bar with a stellar outlook. Enjoy fish and chips on the beach for dinner or rise above it all with some bold top-end cuisine. Spend the rest of the evening kicking on at an outdoor festival or catching a performance at the Opera House. Any good night in Sydney ends with a 3am 'I can't believe I just ate that' pie floater experience, sitting with the seagulls at Harry's Café de Wheels in Woolloomooloo.

}

ALTHOUGH MIRIAM HAS SPENT MUCH OF THE LAST FEW YEARS ON THE ROAD, THE SUN-KISSED DELIGHTS OF HER HOME-TOWN SYDNEY KEEP DRAWING HER BACK: snorkelling with the groupers at Gordon's Bay, long afternoon barbeques with mates in the park and dancing until she drops at all-day music festivals. Weekends involve wandering the lively outdoor markets in search of vintage clothing or fresh produce to cook up a storm in her inner-city apartment. Late evenings, film and writers festivals, early morning swims and Sundays in Chinatown are some of her favourite things.

PHOTO CREDITS

}

CITIESCAPE
SYDNEY

OCTOBER 2006

**PUBLISHED BY LONELY PLANET
PUBLICATIONS PTY LTD**
ABN 36 005 607 983
90 Maribyrnong St, Footscray,
Victoria 3011, Australia
www.lonelyplanet.com

Printed through Colorcraft Ltd, Hong Kong.
Printed in China.

PHOTOGRAPHS
Many of the images in this book are available
for licensing from Lonely Planet Images.
www.lonelyplanetimages.com

ISBN 1 74104 933 4

© Lonely Planet 2006
© photographers as indicated 2006

LONELY PLANET OFFICES
AUSTRALIA Locked Bag 1, Footscray, Victoria 3011
Telephone 03 8379 8000 Fax 03 8379 8111
Email talk2us@lonelyplanet.com.au

USA 150 Linden St, Oakland, CA 94607
Telephone 510 893 8555 TOLL FREE 800 275 8555
Fax 510 893 8572 Email info@lonelyplanet.com

UK 72–82 Rosebery Ave, London EC1R 4RW
Telephone 020 7841 9000 Fax 020 7841 9001
Email go@lonelyplanet.co.uk

Publisher ROZ HOPKINS
Commissioning Editor ELLIE COBB
Editors JOCELYN HAREWOOD, VANESSA BATTERSBY
Design MARK ADAMS
Layout Designer INDRA KILFOYLE
Image Researcher PEPI BLUCK
Pre-press Production GERARD WALKER
Project Managers ANNELIES MERTENS, ADAM MCCROW
Publishing Planning Manager JO VRACA
Print Production Manager GRAHAM IMESON